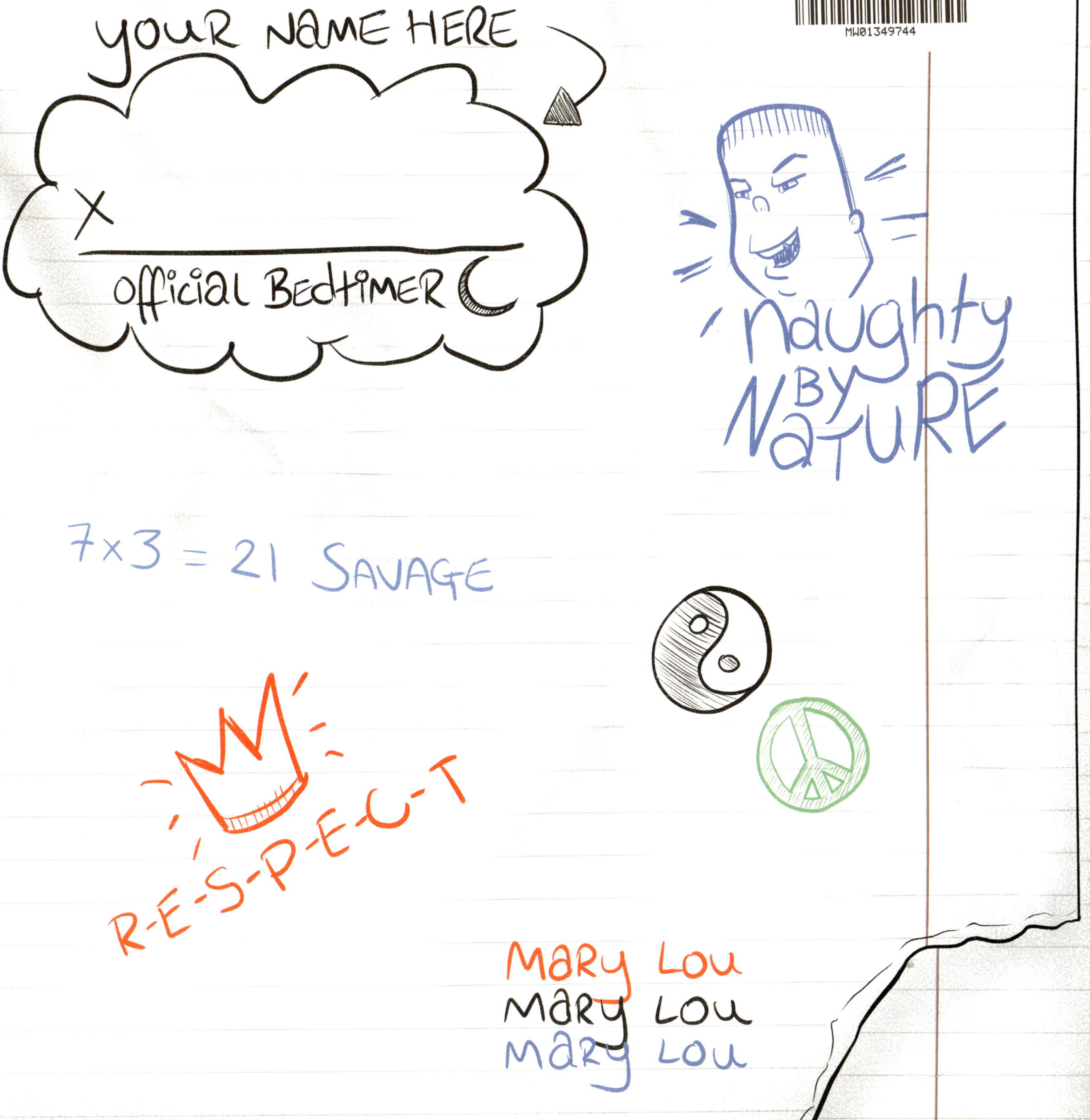

YOUR NAME HERE
X_____
official Bedtimer

naughty BY NaTURE

7×3 = 21 SAVAGE

R-E-S-P-E-C-T

Mary Lou
Mary Lou
Mary Lou

THE BEDTIME CHRONICLES

GIRL WITH THE BLUE HAIR

Written By
Derek Siskin

Illustrated By
Jamie Sale

The Bedtime Chronicles: Girl With The Blue Hair
Copyright © 2021 Derek Siskin

Co-created by Ryan Alovis
Illustrated by Jamie Sale
Art direction by Derek Siskin
Cover design and formatting by C.S. Fritz

All rights reserved under the Pan-American and International Copyright Convention. This book may not be reproduced in whole or in part, except for the brief quotations embodied in critical articles or reviews, in any form or by any means, electronic or mechanical, including photocopying, recording, or by any information storage and retrieval system now known or hereinafter invented, without permission of the author.

For more information: www.thebedtimechronicles.com
ISBN: 978-1-7367274-1-6
Printed in PRC

To my Grandma Joyce Lowenstein for being an inspiration to everyone
who knows her and showing us that with the right mindset,
we can accomplish anything.

To Mylo and Freddy, being your dad is the greatest joy of my life.
May you always stay true to yourself, treat others with respect,
and follow your heart wherever it might lead you.

- DS

To my amazing children, Sophia, Austin & Emilee, forgive me for the
embarrassment you're about to receive while I attempt to rap this book
to you in our monotonously uncool English accent.

- JS

PREPARE TO RHYME

READ OR RAP

IT'S YO BEDTIME

My name is Benny and that's my sister Mary Lou,

I'm five years old, Mary's eight, and her hair is blue.

This is my bunny, we like to call him Hip-Hop,
he's pretty chill hence the shades and the flip-flops.

My mom is Pam, my dad is Stan – short for Stanley, and now I've told you 'bout the whole Rimes family.

Anyways, the day is done so before I get all snore'y, you bet your butt I wanna hear a bedtime story.

Hmm... you wanna know the story why my hair is blue?

You know I do.

It came about because a dude was very rude.

With you know who.

I caught a 'tude and then my mood started to brew.

And then it grew.

And what ensued turned out to be a little feud.

With Mary Lou!

See it all started with a dare from Bobby Shay,
this boy in class who always has something to say.

Okay okay.

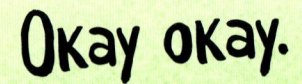

And then he said that pink's for girls and blue's for boys,
and that they're smarter, stronger, faster - all that noise.
I said you're wrong and did my best not to lose it.

Pump the breaks!

Then Bobby Shay got in my face and told me, "Prove it."

Big mistake.

We started with a simple game of tic-tac-toe.
I beat him seven straight times in a row.

X's and O's!

And finally I took him down to the track,
100 meter beat him while I ate a snack.

A cracker jack.

Cause everybody's different with a different view.
It's like a rainbow and we're each a different hue.

You tell 'em Lou!

And then I thought about the marker and I knew.
I wanted to remind myself what I'd been through.
To always know there are no dreams I can't pursue.
So that's the reason why I dyed my hair blue.

Truuuuue!

Now cozy up and get some rest because it's bedtime.

You got it sis - c'mon Hip-Hop, until the next rhyme.

Derek Siskin is the author of *The Bedtime Chronicles*. The first release of the series, *Legend of the Dadman*, captured the imaginations of families who enjoy a good story, some hip-hop vibes, and the occasional fart joke before bedtime. When he's not dropping the hottest children's book verses of all time, Derek lives with his wife and kids on the tropical oasis known as Long Island, NY.

Jamie Sale is an illustrator and cartoonist from the UK who speaks with a funny English accent. His amazing children, Sophia, Austin & Emilee have played a huge role in making him the man he is today, a penniless artist. After having so much fun creating *Legend of the Dadman*, it didn't take much to coax Jamie into illustrating this next book of the series – except for promises of fame and fortune of course.